A Winter Journey

A Winter Journey

Semine

ΤΗΙ ΚΑΛΛΙΣΤΗΙ
Til min Elskede

You have been through so much.
But you are here Now.

Here to be honoured for
your Strength,
your Softness,
your Wisdom,
your Beauty,
your Way.

These words are for you
to water your Heart
so that you may heal.

To nourish your Soul
so that you may shine.

To feather your Wings
so that you may fly
–to New Heights.

There is a Place
where you can never be harmed.

She will meet you there.

As she emerged in the
Darkness, she could not see
The Way.

So she had no choice but to
Listen and Trust the Direction.

A Guardian voice of Protection
showed up in the midst of the
Void,

"Don't be afraid of this Journey.
It was never meant to harm
you; you are of Divine Nature."

And her Ancestors chimed in
through distant Whispers,

"You are more than what you
think you have lost. You are
The Way of the New. You are
the Soul of Forever.

"Remember that, and the whole
World will bow to your
Reverence."

It was an Initiation and a Dare, where she was asked to Trust in all that was in store for her.

It only required one tiny little word, one moment, one breath,

"Say Yes."

As she stepped out on the New Ground, it presented itself as the Mountain of Eternity,

"I have been here for Generations before you and will stay long after you. But when you touch me, I will be forever changed."

"The Path will be rocky, but it will lead you to your Treasure. It will teach you to honour your Gifts. It will take you to the Castle of your Ruby coloured Soul, where a flame of Burning Love is waiting for you."

And the North Wind swirled
up around her and asked her to
reclaim her Freedom,

"Lay your Past to rest now and
feel the lightness of being
without any burdens.

"Embrace the Storm with open
arms and feel the Power of
stepping onto The Path of your
New Beginning."

She felt quite afraid and alone and looked for the oldest and tallest Pine tree in the woods for Guidance.

She sat beneath him in the Cold, but He remained silent and asked her to come back another time.

The next day, Pine gave her
Permission and Power to wish
well,

"Don't fear, but tell me what it
is you want. And Dare to let
yourself be held by Mother
Earth like a little Child. Let her
show you how Big Life can be.
Let it unfold.

"Now it is time to walk in
Beauty."

And she courageously walked on, when Water showed up with a Spring who carried Treasures from the Big Sea into a Wishing Well.

Little Shells sparkled to catch her eye as precious messengers to tell her that she was on the Right Way,

"Walk in Circles towards The Top and keep going Up."

Day became Night and the
Wind became strong, and she
stopped to simply sit and listen:

To the Strength and Power of
Mother Nature. It was like a
Song from her Childhood that
sent her into Dreamtime.

She dreamt about something
ancient.

Creation Energy.
Honour.
Hope.
Humanity.

As an Invitation and a Dare to
retreat into her own Sacred
Space.

And she decided to let Time
have her way with her.

To let the Darkness cocoon her
in Comfort and Protection.

To let her Ashes be kissed by
her Blessings and be
transformed into the Golden
Dust of her New Wings.

She felt cold, but remembered
the Promises.

She learned that each Season
has its own Wisdom.

She learned to sit in the
Darkness of Winter.

To allow the Stars in the sky to
guide The Way.

As she laid her Loss and
Sorrow to rest like Seeds in the
ground and watered them with
her tears, a Promise was made
to her,

"Something will grow from
these Seeds. Wait and see."

"How can Something grow
from Nothing," she reasoned.

"How could Anything arrive by
letting go."

And the waxing Winter Moon
showed her,

"Do nothing and let Patience
transform you into a New State.

"Think of the Miracle of
Spring.

"Be the Butterfly."

And a Hemisphere of twinkling Stars watched over her, as she rested in Dreamtime, igniting the Stars within her, one by one.

Suddenly, something inside her
was kindled.

A Light in her Heart.

A Spark in her Eyes.

A slow-burning Flame
of Glow-in-the-Dark.

And she woke up to a string of
Sunshine that welcomed her
into a New Day.

It was like a Path of Light that
she dared to Dance in.

When she listened to her New
Body, she could really feel It:

What felt Right and Wrong.
What was Good for her.
What she Needed.
What she Longed for.
What gave her Comfort and
made her feel Safe.

And suddenly, she knew it was time to unfold her New Wings of Trust and Dare in awe of her Magic Dust.

And she understood how
Blessed she was.

Not only had she met
another kind of Beauty.

She had met the Sacredness of
the Dark.

She had been given
a New Home.
A New Land.

She had been invited into an
everlasting Adventure of
Endless Love.

Bit by bit, day by day, she claimed the Land of her Sovereignty.

Guided on the Path by magical breadcrumbs, she walked into her New Territory on hallowed Ground.

As she began her Song with the
Words in her Heart, she heard
the Echo of a distant voice,

"Yes, I love you like Life itself.

My Dignity.
My Humanity.
My Prosperity.
The Land of my Future.

"Yes, I bow to you."

And she decided to build
a New Home for herself.
And for Others.

This time, she would take her
time to feel the Instructions.
Not rush. But respect the
Wisdom Journey.

As she put all her Teachings to use, she found a New Power.

Not only could she feel Places and Pathways, but the Doors of Life opened to her on their own.

And the Gates opened to the
Palace of her own Heart.

How Vast it was,
how Big,
how Loving,
how Tender.

What a Kingdom to be the
Empress of.

This place felt like Home.

Around and around, she had
travelled only to find the
Centre of all she had ever
wanted inside herself.

Love,
Peace,
Grace.

In the Garden of her
Homecoming.

Here she found another Time
Zone. Away from the race.

And she entered the Castle of
her Soul with so many Rooms
to explore.

Sadness,
Tenderness,
Bliss,

each holding different Wisdom
for different Moments.

As she had befriended her New
Dare, she stepped out on her
New Land:

An endless Meadow, where the
Grass was gracefully swaying,
and the sky was Ablaze with the
colour of Burning Love.

In the twinkling of an Eye, she
heeded the call on the Horizon,

"There is a way for you to
Pioneer."

"Child of
the perfect Winter Storm.

"Passing Mountains.
Melting Snowflakes.
Finding Way.

"Live for Them.
Love for Them.

"Show Them Home."

And She will give you Everything,
you will ever need.

And you shall be Safe and Protected on
your Journey.

About the Author

Sidsel Solmer Eriksen is an artist and writer living in Copenhagen, Denmark.

She mirrors human seasons through nature's cycles, elements and forces within a nature-rooted worldview that invites humanity to reconnect with the voice, wisdom and medicine of Mother Earth.

An award-winning creative director, she has worked internationally, published an independent art magazine, and written and illustrated a children's book.

A Winter Journey is a poetic tale of her own Dark Night of the Soul, which began with a diagnosis of stage IV uterine cancer in 2020. As part of her healing journey, she turned to nature therapy and the sacred practice of the Medicine Walk — a path that guided her towards healing and a new way of living.

May you, or someone dear to you, find refuge and solace in these words as you walk your own Winter Journey.

You can find more of her words and works at seminejourney.com.